My Very First Alphabet Book

JayCee Publications

Copyright © JayCee Publications, 2020

All rights reserved.

No part of this publication may be reproduced, distributed, or transmitted in any form or by any means, including photocopying, recording, or other electronic or mechanical methods, without the prior written permission of the publisher.

ISBN-13: 978-0-9689408-6-0

Publisher:

JayCee Publications
Brampton, Ontario, CANADA

Jaspal.Cheema@gmail.com
416-573-2164

Availability:

This book is also available from www.Amazon.com and several other Amazon websites. Check your local Amazon website. In Canada, for example, it is available from www.Amazon.ca

Photo Credits:

All images in this book are used under license from Shutterstock.com

Graphic Layout & Design: Jaspal Singh Cheema

Acknowledgements:

I'd like to thank my two boys—Herman and Gurman Cheema—for their invaluable input in the preparation of this book. I'd also like to thank Mr. Akashdeep Singh Pannu for his technical advice and guidance. Their assistance is greatly appreciated.

A big THANK YOU to my friend, Suresh Kalia, who never holds anything back while offering downright impartial, unbiased, and pragmatic advice.

Big A

Little a

Apple

Ant

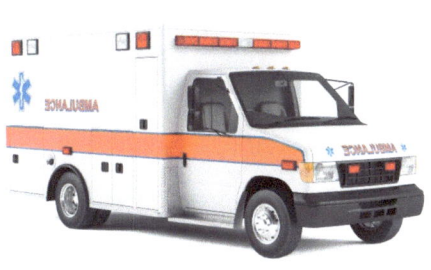
Ambulance

Apricot

Almonds

Alligator

Big B  **Little b**

Baby

Banana

Butterfly

Bear

Broccoli

Balloon

Big C · Little c

Cat · Candy

Cake · Car

Clown · Cow

Big D

Little d

Dog

Doughnut

Dragonfly

Dolphin

Dinosaur

Doll

Big E

Little e

Elephant

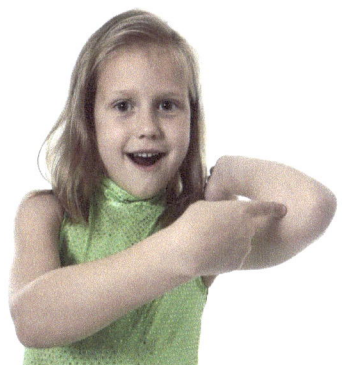
Elbow

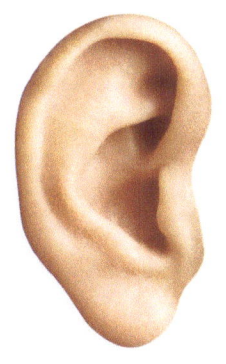
Ear

Elk

Eye

Eagle

Big F

Little f

Frog

Fish

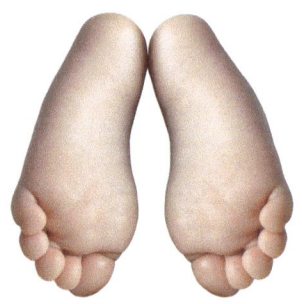
Feet

Fox

Flower

Fly

Big G — **Little g**

Grapes — **G**orilla

Giraffe — **G**oat

Gloves — **G**uitar

Big H

Little h

Horse

Hen

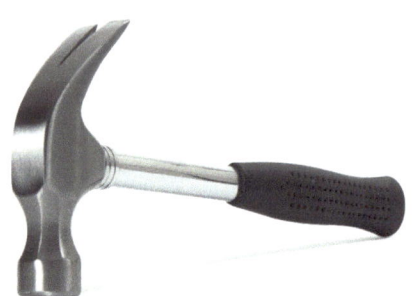
Hammer

Honey

Hand

Hat

Big I **Little i**

Iguana Igloo

Ice Cream Iron

Iris Island

Big J   **Little j**

Jaguar   **J**ello

Jam   **J**acket

Jet   **J**ellyfish

Big K   **Little k**

Kangaroo   **K**ite

Key   **K**itten

Kiwi   **K**ingfisher

Big L **Little l**

Leaf **L**adybug

Lemur **L**emon

Lime **L**ion

Big M

Little m

Mouse

Mittens

Monkey

Marbles

Mango

Macaw

Big N

Little n

Nest

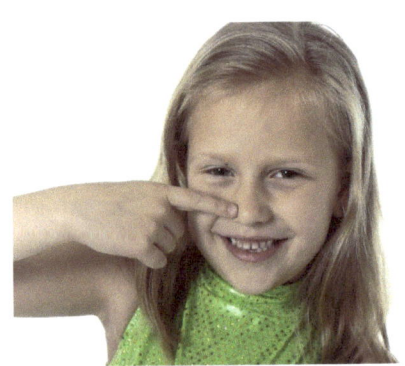
Nose

Necklace

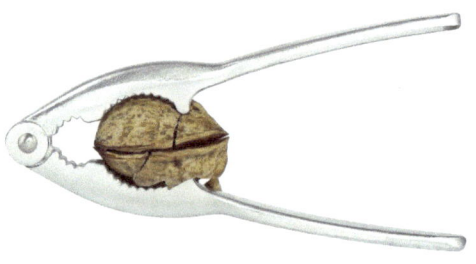
Nutcracker

Nails

Nailcutter

Big P **Little p**

Pizza **P**arrot

Pigeon **P**uppy

Penguin **P**ineapple

Big Q — Little q

Queen — Quilt

Question Mark — Quince

Quail — Quartz

Big R

Little r

Rabbit

Radish

Rooster

Rhinoceros

Raspberry

Raisins

Big S **Little s**

Snail **S**nake

Scorpion **S**trawberry

Sheep **S**quirrel

Big T   **Little t**

Tree   **T**iger

Tomato   **T**urtle

Toucan   **T**arantula

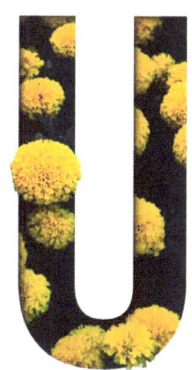
Big U

Little u

Umbrella

Undershirt

Ukulele

Urinal

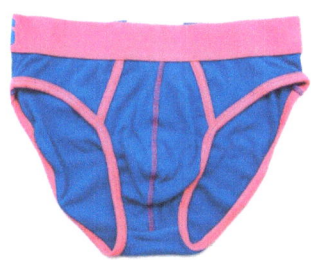
Underwear

Big VLittle v

VultureVan

ViolinVacuum Cleaner

VegetablesVase

Big W   **Little w**

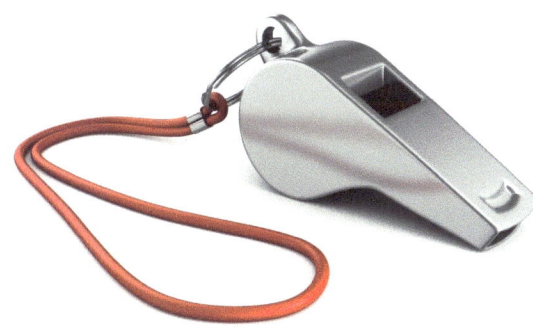 

Whistle   **W**alnut

Watermelon   **W**heelbarrow

Woodpecker   **W**olf

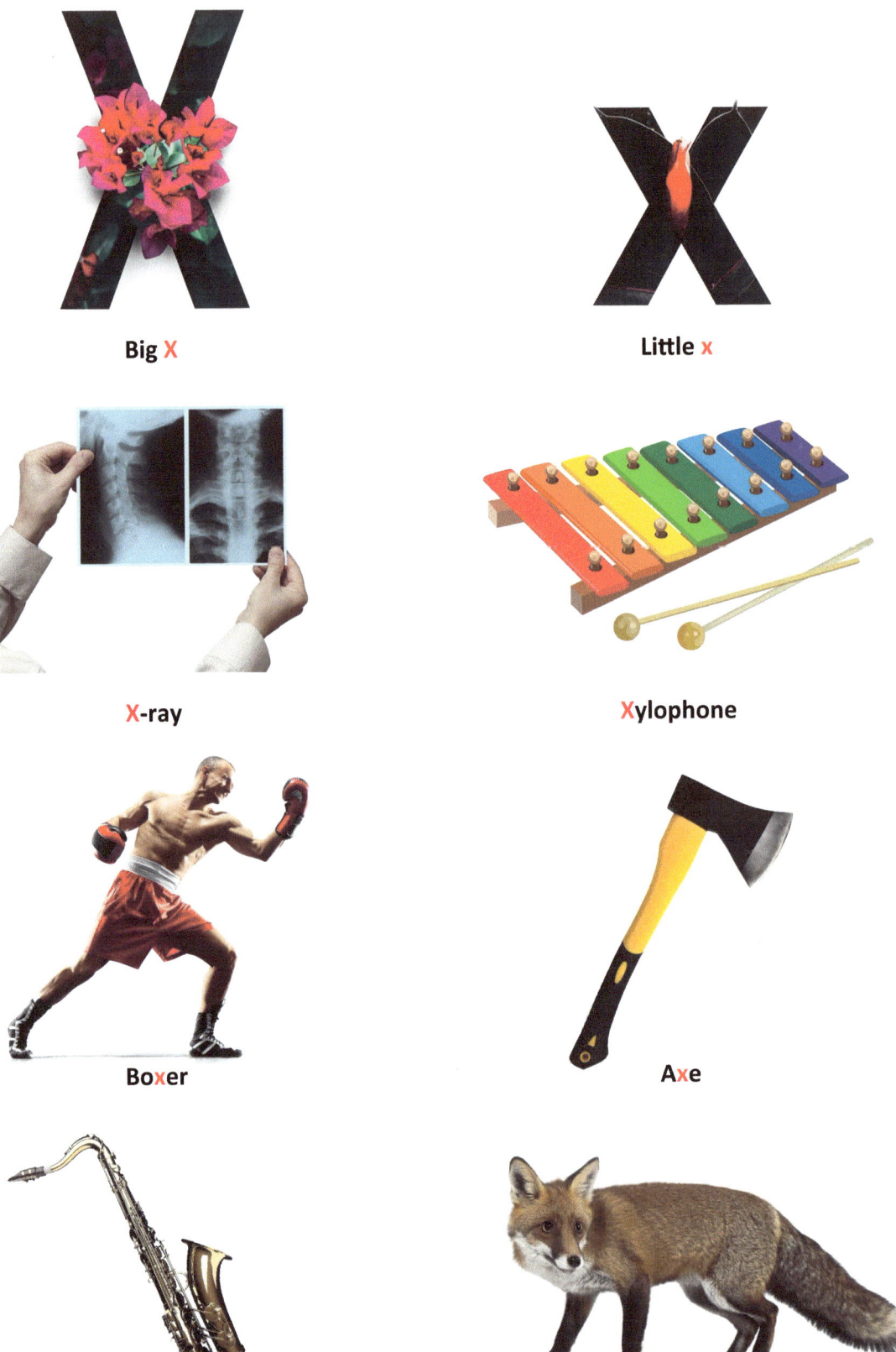

Big X

Little x

X-ray

Xylophone

Bo**x**er

A**x**e

Sa**x**ophone

Fo**x**

Big Y   **Little y**

Yo-Yo   Yak

Yarn   Yeast

Yacht   Yam

Big Z   **Little z**

Zebra   **Z**ipper

Zero   **Z**ucchini

One  Wolf

Two  Tigers

Three  Ladybugs

Four 4 Feathers

Five **5** Foxes

Six  Snails

Seven 7 Spiders

Nine  Nurses

Ten 10 Trees

We are done!

www.ingramcontent.com/pod-product-compliance
Lightning Source LLC
Chambersburg PA
CBHW040035050426
42450CB00024B/66